Energeticum/ Phantasticum

ΕNERGETICUM / PHANTASTICUM:

a Profane Epyllion
in Seven Cantos

by Tom Bradley

MadHat Press
MadHat Incorporated
PO Box 8364, Asheville, NC 28814

Portions of this book have appeared in *The Journal of Poetics Research,
Danse Macabre,* and *Quarterday Review.*

The Library of Congress has assigned
this edition a Control Number of
2016963061

ISBN 978-1-941196-41-0 (paperback)

Cover art and design by Marc Vincenz
Author portrait by David Aronson
alchemicalwedding.com
Book design by MadHat Press

www.MadHat-Press.com

First Printing

Contents:

The Spiral Goddess assumes the shape of Wayne Newton, the Midnight Idol, whose music is hopelessly lucid, but whose voice and person exude the opposite quality to an hallucinatory degree. A walking *phantasticvm*, Wayne recapitulates the spirit-body hermaphroditism of Hans Christian Andersen in Canto Two. He closes off the show with a guest appearance, live from Las Vegas. Honest heathenism has triumphed!

CANTO 1.
ARGUMENT:

The Abrahamic God's eternality, but not his
existence, is debunked. He is shown to be the
Demiurge, boastful, insane and blind, with
an unpleasant odor. A pair of contemporary
Neo-Atheists who smell nothing are reduced
to little boys and tucked into their bunk-bed
for the night. They suffer lucid dreams of
Roman beast wranglers and concentration-camp
matrons hiding in the closet.

*I*n eighteen-fifty-five, *era vulgaris,*
   a goyish magus with the pseudonym
of Frater Eliphas Levi was inspired
to hear, transcribe and bruit along the Seine
5 *Le Dogme de la Haute Magie Ancienne.*
And in the prolegomenon he aired,
with all its talismanic *bric-à-brac,*
the emblematic monster of your age,
your default thing that bumps you in the night.

10   The Frater serenades us with this choir:

    That phantom of all theogonic terrors,
that dragon Persians know as Ahriman,
that Typhon of Nilotic Hierophants,
that Python which the Greeklings anagrammed,
15 *that serpent charmed by Israelitish tribes,*
that baby-ravishing Croquemitaine,
that gargoyle who eructates molten lead,

Nineteenth-Century
Europe's greatest occultist
comes forward with a
curiously inexhaustive
catalogue of demons. A famous
name is not to be found.

1

that beast the Middle Ages loved to dread,
and—worse than these—the Templars' Baphomet!
20   The alchemistic idol with the beard!
Old Mendes' deity, obscenely drunk!
The billy goat in Sabbath orgies sunk!
The figure of the Emperor of Night,
with all his attributes and equipage!
25   A chimera, a sphinx, a thinking blight,
a synthesis of all deformities!

Does this intimidating catalogue
seem short one boogeyman or bugaboo?
Whose moniker is missing from the muster,
30   the biggest name of all, for half the world,
from Middling Orient to San Berdoo?

Examine every grim particular   *A perusal of Eliphas Levi's*
made manifest in Levi's frontispiece: *illustration is undertaken, to*
A goat's head, with its horns, its floppy ears, *identify the absent entity.*
35   its beard, conjoined to form the pentagram
Republicans have crassly vulgarized,
impaling it upon a single point.
We see an eagle's wings, your mother's breasts,
a scaled caduceus that feigns to fill
40   Hermaphrodite's ithyphallic part.
And, waving in the thick mephitic air,
lascivious and semen-slippery hands:
the Archbishop's two-fingered benediction.

You, theist, can you tell me who this is,   *The theist is interrogated,*
45   though his horrendous handle goes unwhispered? *resulting in identification*
Your orthodoxy's widespread prejudice   *of the anonymous fiend's*
would make his *nom de plume* subsume the roll. *opponent.*
You'd coronate the paragraph with horns

and all the other aliases suborn,
50   a laundry list of scary sobriquets.

    You'd puff this nonspecific angel up
to magnify his formidable foe:
his hypertrophied arch-nemetic rival,
butch Superman to his enflamed Lex Luthor.
55   Your unnamed spookling stomps the rosin box
to square against the biggest spook of all,
his partner, all-but-equitably-matched:

    Cue God, with an emphatic capital *Gee!*

    To spar with One and Only Supreme Beings,
60   you need to let this catchy-sounding tag
be sequined on your spandex stretchy pants:
*The Absolute Eternal Principle
of Endless Evil Unadulterate.*
Red Satan is a smashing novelty act.
65   So why would Europe's greatest magian
disdain him in that mighty *chef d'oeuvre,
Le Dogme de la Haute Magie Ancienne?*

Yahweh's coeval antagonist is named. The question of Lucifer's neglect by esoteric adepts is directly posed.

    A mind unprecedented of its kind
has coagulated out of sheer aether
70   throughout the latest two millennia.
In human history's overlong context,
this mental mutant comes off more grotesque
than Abigail and Brittany Hensel rolled
in one décolletaged and skin-tight singlet.
75   Distinguished megalomaniacally,
its sense of self's enflamed and crusted over
with growths apparent as the Elephant Man's.
This monstrous self will look upon the world

The question begins to be addressed, with introduction of the type of mind in which eternality and existence don't mutually exclude. The anomaly of that world-view is exposed.

to presuppose a somewhat larger Self:
80   the Sole Proprietor and CEO,
the Licensor and Manufacturer
of Abso-God-Damned-Lutely Everything.

When first confronted by this brain infarct,
the Romans were so flustered, they recoiled
85   in self-defense, enlisting carnivores.
Carpophorus the *bestiarius*,
the Empire's master wrangler, hustled lions
(and, even more effectively, mastiffs)
to dine upon some homonotic vectors
90   of the large and lonely God bacterium.
And later, in a camp near Buchenwald,
the *Oberaufseherin* quarantined
descendants of the folks who would be blamed
for incubating God's original strain.

Two historical examples of extreme reactions to adherents of the One God.

95   These days, with skeptical modernity's
soul-killed and chloroformed metaphysique,
this God is bearded as a vaporous freak.
Dead Hitchens and Dick Dawkins thump their sternums
to moot the only two alternatives
100   discussable in their cosmology.
On one hand, they inform us, fearlessly,
there sucks a spirit vacuum round the Earth
more nearly perfect than the void of space,
as it contains no dark material.
105   (Smart money's giving odds on that denial.)
The other hand shoves forth this grand burlesque,
this narcissistic Abrahamic tool.

Two famous contemporary neo-atheists are roused from their spiritual and intellectual slumber, to be skewered

Their inadequate monism is ridiculed.

The crazed Aghori mendicant who gnaws
cremations on a Varanasi ghat;

4

110 the Shivwit squaw who, mescalinical,
will waltz her red bliss in the Utah sand;
the chaste Theosophist whose ragas move
his fellows on the Pasadena bench;
the salary-man of Òsaka, sardined
115 on bullet trains a full three hours each day:
these honest heathens would dismiss your Dawk,
your dead Hitch, and their dialectic, too,
as, on one hand, counterintuitve,
and weirdly infantile upon the other.
120 And so would Monsieur Eliphas himself,
our universal *Prisca Theologve*.

The amused, if puzzled, reaction of honest heathens to dead Christopher Hitchens and Richard Dawkins.

"A spirit vacuum," did those atheists shrill?
In all the ancient towns and times until
Descartes' emission of nocturnal doubt
125 that marred his weekend on the blue Danube,
all people knew the air is flocked with souls,
as Jewish Philo sang in *On the Giants*.
Not just the air, but dirt, and flame and rain
still pullulate promiscuously with Mind
130 and tendrils of anthropic consciousness,
a good proportioning of whom would loom
too monstrously for uninitiate eyes.

In orders, ranks and sub-varieties
come Limniads, Pookas, Clurichauns and Sylphs.
135 Their antic universe resembles zilch
if not a gander down a microscope
at dribbles eye-dropped from some hidden ditch,
or Erythrèan scuba videos
shot by Fatima's sons, the Hashemites,
140 whose Board of Tourism would exorcise
the seaweed-swirling Gulf of Aqaba.

A fluid bestiary of the once universal Prisca Theologia, or original heathen religion.

5

Amoebas, sea slugs, gryphons with wet wings
in clouds arise from Mussulmannish seas
to jam our telescopes, our lungs, our minds
145   with superfine materiality.

As far as old Jehovah goes, that oaf,
how does he swim in honest heathens' view?
Luxuriating Hindu corpse devourer,
do you demur, like atheism's shills,
150   to entertain that bully's *existence*?
(The operative word to keep in mind.)
You blissful peyotistic Amerind,
you theosophizing Californian saint,
you son of Shinto godling Hirohito—
155   each member of my pagan-eyed quartet,
will you now register, with full consent,
this creature's vast ineffability
among the rolls of Philo's unseen rascals?

Right-thinkers from the Indian subcontinent, the New World and the Extreme Orient are asked this question: how, if at all, and where, would Jehovah fit into their crowded atmosphere?

They welcome God as Cobweb did the weaver!
160   They make him wear again the floppy ears
of that donkey-phallused, *hee-haw*-braying honyock
whose Solomonic liturgy was aired
by Posidonius the Japhethite.
His skull, exuding asininity,
165   Antiochus the Fourth Epiphanes
uncovered in the Levites' shut precincts
when scouring out Sanctum Sanctorum's sink,
just as the Templars later plied as "god"
a bestial noggin, from the rubble dug
170   while camping at the mosque called Al-Aqsa.

A goblin among goblins, the Lord of Abraham is embraced—at arm's length, due to body odor.

Certain classical pagans and Medieval Knights familiarized themselves with the bestial nature of God at the source.

With horns and beard and gritty cranium,
God makes the most obnoxious wraith of all,

the biggest goblin with the worst B.O.,
the crass Dubya–Obama of the clan.

175 Señor Miguel Serrano, prophet, seer
of Esoteric Hitlerism's faith,
calls Heavenly Father "Plagiarist Demiurge,"
while Valentinians wince as he miscarries
within the wizened womb of Sophia.

180 Insane and boastful, blind and none too bright
is our Unitary-style Executive.
"I'm the decider," says the jealous cob.
"Above me thou shalt have no thicker clods."

Speak of devils, now's propitious time
185 for one non-monster to appear—or *dis-*.
Xenophanes of Colophon says this:

One god there is, in no way like a creature,
not formed in body nor in cast of mind.
Its wholeness thinks, its wholeness hears, it stays
190 *perpetually motionless in space.*
It wields all things by wishing without will.

In Christendom and thereabouts, this Mind,
immobile, immaterial, too fine,
is, without fail, bemuddled and misknown
195 as monotheism's ass upon a throne.
But monsters fade without deformity,
and deformation squawks for attributes.
And what is Satan's rival but a wad
of attributes, all lumpy as a gnome's?

200 When coming close as humanly you can
to glimpsing deep Xenophanes' sole cipher;
when grasping at the barest naked hint

He is not the loveliest sprite.
But his grossness suits him for
the heavy, smelly sweat-work
of material creation.

A pre-Socratic philosopher
begins gently to introduce us to
the true Ultimate Reality, as
opposed to the Man Upstairs,
for whom it's perennially
mistaken.

Hints of Unthinkable That's
sheer sublimity.

7

of unrecorded Akasha's pure naught;
when down your brain so briefly drains the drop,
205 the adumbrated emanating zero
sub-continentals silently call *That*,
you cannot help but in your bowels abhor
unsubtle, gross, theistic blasphemy.
You understand the Romans' rationale
210 for feedings in their meaty Coliseum,
where Christers rendered livers unto Nero
to cheer the Jerry-rigger of the Earth.

Monotheism is sacrilege taken beyond the point of paranoid schizophrenia. No level of repugnance it inspires can be too extreme.

To tart the botched Creator Monster up
and fob him off as Ultimately Real;
215 to plunge the limbless *That Unthinkable*
to its red elbows in Saharan dearth,
in genocidal wars, in AIDS obstetrics—
theodicies that drive practitioners
of priestcraft to dysfunctionality
220 while catechizing prolapsed acolytes—
must boil down to mythopoetic sloth,
imagination's paralytic sleep,
among the sons of Shem and cults they spawned.

Intimate relationship is exposed between "Our Father which art in Heaven" and the sickest abuses of his pedophiliac priestcrafters.

Someone, having hands to get besmirched
225 with world creation's work, will have a name;
and, being named, or even briefly thought,
exists as much as his parishioners.
Eventually he rots, like arms and legs
of children flayed and tattooed by the bitch
230 of Buchenwald, the *Oberaufseherin*.
Götterdämmerung's unbordered by Bayreuth.

The necessarily material, and hence ephemeral, nature of Our Maker.

To those who read the Bible narratives
correctly—that's to say, between the lines

as veiled and esoteric mysteries—
235   a fine familiar tune is sharply sung
in this brief unsynoptic Gospel clause
recorded by the most Beloved Disciple:

> *Believing in one God, the devils tremble.*

The right interpretation of this passage
240   will yield some wisdom to your opened ear:
the *Prisca Theologically* clued-in
are nowhere near as superstition-cowed
as devils' fatuous species. That includes
grotesqueries, demonically ordained,
245   who prance behind the pulpit while they preach,
believe and tremble, like their hellish kin,
and spasm in embroidered chasubles,
small bishops genuflecting in the midst.

Aleister Crowley, Baphomet himself,
250   must say it better than Saint John the Maiden:

> *Vulgarians see naught past the Creator.*

So, open up your gut and let God in.
He'll be the bitch of your own Buchenwald;
the *bestiarius* who goads the ox
255   that buggers you to death in the arena;
the biggest bogey trundling down our road,
three hundred pounds of drooler on the bus,
across the littered aisle from where you cower,
the one with transubstantiated chalice
260   he elevates from folds of unctioned raincoat.

Stay calm, don't look at him, pretend he's vapor.

You don't want him asperging you with banter.
Just contemplate my hymn upon your lap
and wait to disembark with all dispatch,
265   but cooly, at the next stop on the schedule,
when time to shuffle off this mortal shuttle.

But, Christ, whatever else you choose to do,
don't lay my lovely book aside to fish
apotropaic grimoires from your purse.
270   Don't chant the syllables of Eliphas,
and don't invoke God's rival's dread nicknames.
That Ritual of Transcendental Magic
encourages this most vain Plasmator
to think his godhead's taken seriously.

Further caution against engaging in ceremonial magic as proselytized by Frater Eliphas Levi.

275   However, never doubt he wields percentage
of omnipotent, omniscient omnipresence,
those qualities deemed proper to that Being
whose primum-mobilized Supremacy
he'd knock you on your knees to praise him for.
280   And, cheek to jowl by us, he edges closer
to timelessness that priestcraft claims for him,
extends unto his "foe eternal," too,
in the holy name of targeted promo.

The Demiurge is our physical superior, and happens to have muddled together our coats of skin; but he has nothing to do with our eternal moiety.

But what, if anything at all, and why
285   should mensurable advantage signify?
Señor Serrano's plagiarist Demiurge
might well have mucked us golems from the mud,
and set us, squirming, sinning, alongside
bestiarius and *Oberaufseherin,*
290   but he didn't insufflate our living lungs,
nor gastrulate our hovering astral monads.
We beneficiaries, and we dupes,

of his glutinous colloidal dispensation
might be his brats, his brawling bottom bitches,
295 but not his feats of fine legerdemain.
We owe him nothing other than back pain,
post-nasal drip, hangnails and eyelid twitches.

Along the margins of the Himalayas
live Brahmans who have memorized the Vedas,
300 who, with a single thought, can atomize
the universe and all its catalogues
of garishly tricked-out Creator-Gods.
Meanwhile, our local knock-off Aryans,
Dick Dawkins and dead Hitchens, take their cue
305 from eight year olds with average IQs.

They're tucked into their bunk-bed for the night,
averring loud that Buchenwald's blond beast
is nowhere in the closet, nor bides time
till lights go out, tattooing dagger inked.
310 The "spirit vacuum" yawns about the bedroom
while sleepless Dawk announces to the dark:
Carpophorus the *bestiarius*
lurks not at *Oberaufseherin*'s side.
The Roman wrangler's favorite rutting rhino
315 won't stretch the leash, unappetized to sniff
dead Hitchens' clothes with disemboweling nose.

Keep talking, boys, don't worry about a thing.

The ultimate power of the perfected human mind, embodied in learned Brahmans, can extinguish the so-called Heavenly Father in a mere afterthought. This is contrasted to Neo-Atheism's timorous childishness.

11

CANTO 11.

ARGUMENT:

Lucid dreaming conduces to the twin insanities of Monotheism and Atheism. Periodic immersion in the abyss of the unmonitored unconscious is a condition of mental and spiritual hygiene. The unseen godlings who inhabit that illucid world are paraded forth in all their beautifully bizarre variety. Hans Christian Andersen presents himself as both vector of lucidity's disease and its antidote, a conjoined hermaphroditic twin of the spirit-body.

W hen secret psychodramas of the night
     initiate us in their mysteries,
320 a blindfold's tourniquetted and cinched tight
to swaddle up our eyes like infant twins
until they're ready to contain a glimpse
of chaos that surpasses all restraint.

    The Lucid Dream will prematurely tease
325 that diaper from your exoteric face.

    Tibetans taught this to their fledgling dead
before enduring death-by-Mao instead.
But dream yogins are just as doctrinaire
as Ratzinger in his sedilia chair.
330 And lately, when those Buddhist bardos gleam,
they're reinterpreted as something screened.

    Halfwitted dreams with one shut eye are dreamt,
half-assed hallucinations semi-slept.

Unadulterated dreams are likened to the mystery rites of antiquity, wherein neophytes' eyes were sealed to prevent premature revelations. The sleeper's relinquishment of control analogizes to the blindfold.

The expedient of artificially extending the hypnagogic state interferes with this process.

The visions allegorized in the ancient funerary texts, here exemplified by the Bardo Thodol, have been replaced by the false lucidity of electronic spectacle.

Morons in direct sunlight grow no smarter under the moon.

13

To flatter waking thoughts, we call them "bright."
335 What makes us think they might illumine sleep?

Beneath those liquid crystal molecules
a glimpse of liquidated personhood's
horrific light is yet available.
Pure nothingness still seethes behind those screens
340 in pre- and post-existent harmony.
Dominions, Powers and Principalities
will show us their annihilating truths
unless they're mashed with asininity.

The hidden profundities are still accessible, as always, through discipline, long patience and humility.

The Lucid Dream is self-endorsing, trite.
345 Do we presume to claim ourselves the right
to spread our own ephemerality
like acne sebum, oiling troubled waves
that otherwise dredge monsters up from depths?

The perishable citizen, the dreck
350 that's taken out and dumped when trashed by death,
assuming the high autocratic post
of Overseer General for Dreams,
exerts fastidiousness upon the Realm
where rot's unripe, bizarrerie the norm.

The lucid dreamer is lumped with the petite bourgeoisie and other simians. This creature of a day, this perishable pudding of sperm and ovum, mistakes his own evanescence for a condition of spiritual reality.

The consciousness, the primate's attitude,
355 entangled in its raveling rag of skin,
a function of the gonads' shamelessness,
projects its flesh dependency on thoughts
that under sleep parthenogenerate.

The personality, quotidian,
360 assumes it owes selfhood to parentage
and, therefore, on the masses of the night

obtrudes overt erotic imagery,
which super-egoistic scruples strip
365   of allosomes and raw humanity.

To pass unindividuated time
connective tissue's caused to interlink.
Together two mere wads of stuff butt heads
in furtive concert, toward no nobler end
370   than to bedungeon in organic cells
the sundry sprites who grace the ambient air.

Spirits are only temporarily buttoned in coats of skin. To impute fleshly concerns to them is the shallow hubris of the lucid dreamer.

It's doubtful that an exiled godly being
on temporary basis matter-mired
would call for mingling as prerequisite
375   instead of something far more pertinent
to spirits' unadulterated state:
hermetic isolation, strange, sublime.

Halfhearted plays for eyes with half-shut lids
are mounted without benefit of Id.
380   We're fornicating to a metronome,
restricting holocausts to hookah tubes,
hysteria to sighs of lassitude.
While gutting babies with a laser tool,
we cauterize and disinfect the wounds
385   before we've even had the time to drool.
Why would we want to will away the chance?

Some of the bizarre consequences of imposing human limitations on the entities that abide in non-spaces.

Because his dreams are emceed by himself,
the Lucid Dreamer looks upon the world
to presuppose that slightly larger Self
390   snatched from a breeze: the most perfunctory
and shallow of all semi-gelled conceits.
The Popish Heavenly Father-*cum*-Prot God

is kidnapped from his Bedouin tribal tent
and styled the Ultimate Reality,
395　himself the most egregious specimen
of Lucid Dreamer semi-dreamt by men.

Just as the Lucid Dreamer here below
puts on a prissy chicken-liver show,
a celibate yet generative Lord
400　oviparized a teen's cloacal quim
in soft-boiled porno-mythopoesy,
to violate his own presumptive laws
like a priest transgressing hairless altar boys.

This Demiurgic errand boy, this mope,
405　gets gussied up as pretty as a pope.
To take this bungling spastic fucker-up
of our particular niggling solar clump,
and puff him into That Unthinkable,
unreachable by either praise or blame,
410　entails the sickest blasphemy of all.

The Ultimate Reality would scorn
to implicate its sacrosanctity
in perpetration of the cosmic botch
we childishly refer to as "our world."
415　It's sacrilege, in exclusivity
performable by Lucid Dreaming dross,
the crassest, the most ultra-obvious
of all counterintuitivities.

The stunted sense of immaterial things
420　that hampers him who never deeply sleeps,
whose Lorelei distracts him from dream work,
retards his rationality as well.

The superficiality of the light snoozer metastasizes beyond the bedroom to the larger sphere of existence, where it bumbles into the Abrahamic God and assigns ultimate reality to this mere Jerry-rigger of the solar system.

The paranoid-schizophrenia of Canto One elicits jeers from Xenophanes of Colophon's Sole Cipher.

So, ears unstopped, he entertains beliefs
epitomizing all vulgarities.

425   To dream lucidity is to commit,
in argument as dumb as circular,
theodicies of cosmic tastelessness.
Vicarious atonement is contrived
when foolishness summarily denies
430 rebirth and karma's double principle
that manifestly runs the universe.
Eternal bliss or torment just as long
supplant probation, which justice demands.
That's Lucid Dreaming's tenseful time-yoked error.

*Christianity's barbarisms
include the replacement of
probation with salvation-
damnation, usurping individual
responsibility with Christ on
the cross.*

435   Such asininity necessitates
a spiritual and moral travesty:
the filthy motto puked in Pseudo-Paul's
Epistle to the Hebrews (clearly forged):
Die only once, and afterwards be judged.
440 For this we have the Lucid Dream to curse.

Reincarnation denied.

    As if it's not uncouth enough to try
to make Jehovah chief executive,
the Lucid Dreamer essays to dumb down
our Gnomes, our Undines, Salamanders, Sylphs,
445 our Elementals and their mighty ilk.
The cherub's terror is masked in baby pudge,
the Syrian Monstress forcibly shanghaied
to grace this world of Disneyfied pastel
with attributes originally belched from Hell.
450 Where fins and scales of wadded mud prevailed,
once wedged all round with hexed cuneiform
that hissed profundities as old as towns,
we get a glabrous tweeny's turquoise gown.

*Reduction of the Elemental
Spirits to childish toys.*

*Cosmeticization of the Divine
Ichthyomorph and her eunuch
priesthood.*

Would Atargatis pose for lucid eyes,
455 or would a single brief self-conscious glance
cause more than cock to swell and barf its brains?
Did she employ that fish tail as a tease,
a tickling adjunct to cartoonish tits,
or as cetacean scourge to smash to bits
460 the shivered shrimp boats of the human wits?

Her followers castrate themselves with shards.
Semìramis, her daughter, dorked a horse.
Somehow I doubt she'd be a slickened thing,
pubeless as an Arab's promised Houri,
465 not bald, but depilated, with a scalp
equipped with polyvinyl-chloride coif
and nipples alien to dairy toil.
Gravity's repealed within their ken.

Ostensible pudenda, barbie-dolled,
470 are glossed beneath agenitalic thighs
perpetually pinched in pudency,
tempered to a Virgin Mary blue,
the surface texture purged of macula.

A non-mammalian lower torso bleeds
475 when stroked by fillet knife, but not monthly.
Nigredo's black unshaped lubricity
gets socialized, elucidated, bleached
by exegesis, epidermis-deep.
Erased is *vene varicose*'s bruise,
480 unpuckered the old *striae distensae.*

Hans Christian Andersen broadcasts the chum
whose hookings could delucidate this dream.
His sea hag's loofah bosom suckles worms;

*The author of Den lille havfrue
appears as a type of the
simultaneously lucid and illucid.*

her toothless gob's a feeder for bled frogs.
485 He should have named his ditty after her
and sunk our mermaid in Chthonian bogs.

CANTO III.
ARGUMENT:

*Literary pursuits are shown to be conducive to
the perfidious lucidity condemned in Canto Two.
Music is extolled as illucidity par excellence.
Alexander Nikolayevich Scriabin steps up as
the ideal embodiment of the latter.*

The end of everything is guaranteed,
like jumbo jets seduced into the sea,
to crush you with the sheer avoirdupois
490 of all the lucid scribblers in your row.

The internet's perverse monstrosity,
apocalyptic, without precedent,
must clarify your bleak predicament:
your universe and all the pens it slings
495 are hurtling toward the great blue pencil job:
that Dissolution, promised in Puranas,
as followed by the bookless Night of Brahma.

*Looking forward to the end
of time, described in the
Vishnu Purana as The Great
Dissolution.*

Our barely-average star, dim, nondescript,
another flush-faced zhlub in fizzled crowds,
500 is sinking ever closer to the drain
that gorges on the grim galactic plane.

Those spirits who have managed, more or less,
through dozens of misspent millennia,
with slow metempsychotic momentum,
505 to inch along the gradual incline
from rock to plant to beast to human thing

*The double-braided doctrine
of rebirth-karma, as upheld
in Canto Two, presents a slow
migration of astral monads along
the chain of being. For them the
impending Great Dissolution
amounts to a dire emergency.*

(some blurring that admittedly fine line),
are groping for fistfuls of cognizance,
by means of which they might discharge a smutch
510   of karmic debt, before the closing bell
of Manvantara's all-must-go fire sale.

Overreach can lurch from cerebella's folds
self-consciousness may stretch to self-express.
Slightly fewer publishers than writers
515   out-legion the cramped fiends who, nuts-to-butts
in Gadarene, impacted swinish guts.
And most have opted virtually to oink.

*Wordmongers' carcasses
have been occupied by a
disproportion of these spirits,
who covet the self-awareness
requisite for demerit's
erasure. Their "books" have
proliferated exponentially due
to the internet.*

A broadband of electromagnetic lit
extrusively is shitting past the brim
520   of our ionosphere, with light-sped bulge.
Its propagation fizzles at the brink
of Pluto's outer orbit, where it's mulched
with Adolf Hitler's televised pep rallies.
To parabolic radio telescopes
525   tripodded on the shores of methane lakes
on cratered exomoons, our "published" oeuvre
must seem an oblate, simmering blood blister
distended to the lurid point of bursting.

*The solar system is awash in
particle-waves of promiscuous
"literature," wirelessly
distributed.*

There was a time when poetasters banished
530   to wilderness beyond the Hudson River
could play the simple part of the Essene.
They planned their biblo-retirement
as dignified inurnment, Qumran-style.
But now the sand in which our scrolls are sunk
535   is digital, composed of lone electrons,
uncounted drifts of subatomic egos,
all schizy, split, infertile as the bits

*Looking back to epochs when
aspirations were tethered to
paper.*

of shivered quartz that bring the West Bank dunes,
white-phosphorized, to writhe like salted slugs.

540   It seems that gaggles of the Great Unwashed
are born with—what? A need? It isn't that.
To drink and masturbate and breathe aren't "needs,"
but basic terms of our embodiment.
For artists and for "artists," it would seem,
545   to flush the psyche's no less metabolic.

*Is writing innate to the human
frame, like singing, dancing and
even finger-painting?*

But prose is strange, no less than poesy.
It's natural to posit dancing genes,
or singing chromosomes, or eukarotes
revealing selves in misty Kinkade daubs.
550   We spasmed, howled and smeared our fecal pigments
before *Ardipithecus* slouched along.
The scribble's only served six thousand years—
unless the learned efforts of savants
should add two hundred further centuries
555   imputing lexicality's import
to squiggles hardly noticed at Lascaux,
the faded FaceBook of the paleoliths,
where troglodytes updated lucid dreams.

But is that time enough to Darwinize
560   deoxyribonuclear poetics?
Is it legit prosimian behavior
to tinker with these bits of alphabet?
Do bonobos tweezing termites with a twig
encompass brachiators' range of skills,
565   their book contracts glommed in prognathous jaws?

If you're unurged, unpredisposed to set
deciphered smudges on a flattened plane,

I cannot grasp, but envy and applaud
your inner life's removed sterility,
570 the numbness of your chaste sensorium,
your nightly bumble's illucidity.
So, you and your immaculate, dwindling kind—
God bless your vacant souls—are now released
to gaseous, ignored oblivion.

*Addressing the apparently
minuscule minority of the species
Homo sapiens who don't "author."*

575 As for the novelizing residue,
the essayists, straitjacketed scenarists,
belletrists in the myriads of millions,
the poets paper-trained in "quiet style,"
I urge you rivals to comport in ways
580 that might eventuate in swollen coffers.

Apostrophizing everybody else.

I'm told such inflammation of the purse
unto an exponentialized degree
is made, at least in in theory, possible.
You block, cut, paste and shove your oeuvre up
585 the satellite-engendered fistula
ballooning, bleeding out from your PC,
and hope that it demurs to burst before
the heliopause that limns the spirit void
beyond our blabbing solar system's rim,
590 some umpteen billion miles, plus change, away.

With coffers swollen, hankers for the zilch
of Brahma's Night will vanish from your mind.
Your incarnation's rigmarole will feign
illusory resemblance to a life.
595 You'll rent a parlor that most human beings
would reckon livable (if marginally).
And, acclimated to your coat of skin,
you'll finally develop social skills

*Success can distract one's
attention from the impending
apocalypse, right up until the
last minute.*

to pen the sort of smug complacency
600 that Oprah Winfrey gorges for her canon.
Your words, content-protected and secure,
abide in Kindle's gated neighborhood,
while every other "author" on the web,
upon Creative Commons squatting rough,
605 awaits with terror the coming *Dies Irae*.

And when Puranic Dissolution's qualm
above the West's abyss begins to lour,
its urgency no more to be ignored
nor purpled by success' invidious dusk,
610 I want you worriers of syllabaries
to mend syntactically graphemic ways.
Please cast off lingo's deconstructed yoke,
and follow Music's ultra-light decorum.

*When that last minute arrives,
it will be time to turn away
from poetry, and toward music.*

Slim sandwiches of cellulose and ink
615 displayed, spine-out, on formica veneer,
like e-books pirated upon a screen,
indifferently must reify sheer genius
and dribbling slack-jawed animality.
They do so silently, to neighbors' joy.
620 But every mongrel in the tenement
will testify, and loud, to the contrary,
if you should call your fiddle's foul refrains
"unjustly overlooked and underrated."

Unstuck to page, in pixels undisplayed,
625 unwedged on wads of Tigris mud, unsmeared
on strips of consecrate Punjabi bark,
unpulverized by Brahma's grinding Night,
good Music's aspirations sift in waves
(too often being pseudomorphed, misknown,

*The writer resembles the
ill-equipped lucid dreamer of
Canto Two. Musicians, on the
other hand, are prepared for
the plunge into the illucid abyss
of Brahma's Night.*

630   as particles Theosophists disown).
It can't be fucked, olfacted, misconstrued
myopically, and if it's gustable,
the tunes smack of conceptual metaphor.

Once words are cauterized from your inked minds,
635   I'll show you oinking, knuckle-dragging scribes
a musicker who's never been content
to write and weep in wait for Armageddon.
He'll mount, conduct and play the Antichrist
in his own made-from-scratch Megiddo war.
640   Unfearful to delicudate his dreams,
he calls the bluff of chaos unrestrained,
recruits his own Dominions, and his Powers,
and nihilizing Principalities.

His week-long rite of "omni-art" absorbs
645   the fivefold consciousness, with *mana*'s self
and *dharma* to make Theravada's six.
(Motoric-kinesthetic's done by dance.)
If multisensory, it's agraphemic,
unglyphed: his revelation's played by heart.
650   No racks for scores, but elbow rests with hookahs
will edify his cellists and their comrades.

Scriabin is heralded and introduced.

His fonts are couriers of wine, not sense.
His *sérifs* cling to harps, not consonants.
His poem's unpunctuated but for tambors.
655   His typography is letterpressed in quavers.
His composing stick's a shimmering baton.

I give you Levi's sound proselytizer,
the Frater's man in cranial concert halls:

Alexander Nikolayevich Scriabin!

CANTO IV.
ARGUMENT:

The Mysterium, *Scriabin's apocalyptic rite,*
is staged in the Himalayas, and brought to
fruition. Humanity is annihilated, the universe
vaporized.

660   If literature is glued between matte covers
     or shat upon a dead machine's display,
  Scriabin's mass demands a mighty gorge
  in Himalaya's crystal stratosphere.
  It's celebrated in a protean zone,
665   a cathedral built, or birthed, for the occasion.
  This fane, like unicellular amoebae,
  must writhe and swell, as counterpoint requires.
  Scriabin tells us, "It is not constructed
  of a single stony species, uniform,
670   but modulates with my *Mysterium.*"
  The architecture's further rubberized
  by psychoactive aerosols, plus tints
  projected from a *clavier à lumières.*

The venue's contrived of malleable stuff.

    Typecast in the role of Celebrant,
675   Scriabin rides his lectern in the apse
  of this gaseous and hierophantic temple.
  He goads and taunts an orchestra of thousands
  to scrape augmented sharp-eleven chords.
  Unruly gangs, antiphonal mixed choirs,
680   their eros uncontainable in words,
  regurgitate the Demiurgic ichor
  from larynxes, both super- and subhuman.

The composer himself conducts, like a ship's captain in a typhoon. His borderline mutinous crew comprises gargantuan choruses.

Perspiring, swelling, in the corbelled vaults,
church bells the size of yacht hulls, gold alloyed
685 with electrum from Ezekiel's ecstasy,
are hung from cumulonimbic fixity,
imbued and seeded with twelve metric tons
of benzoin, storax, myrrh, of galbanum,
of yellow sandalwood, of cinnamon,
690 in bonfires kindled by the praying mob,
who, on the seventh day of group orgasm,
become cloudlike themselves, unknowable
from schizotoxic mists that melt the murals.

The air is insane with perfumes and sprayed psychotropic alkaloids (phantastica).

The congregation begins to shed individual identities.

Everything's tympanically tormented
695 by the agonizing Roosky Mystic Chord.
The planetary chassis struggles hard
to free itself from quartile iterations
of C, F-sharp, B-flat, E, A and D.
Promethean feats of devilish technique
700 by Alexander Nikolayevich
absolve parishioners' Purgatorial pique
into a stable F-sharp minor triad.
This sonic normalcy brings down the beat
when congregation, clergy, all commixed,
705 like scent in a boudoir, are atomized.
It's not the Night, but the *Soirée* of Brahma.

Scriabin's dissonances constitute aural probation. Like a vicariously atoning Christ, he takes it upon himself to wrestle and subdue this cacophony into a stable sonority.

This perfect cadence signals and comprises the end of time. The Great Dissolution becomes a Great Resolution.

The mystery achieves Puranic purpose:
humanity's abject annihilation,
and hatching of a wholesome race of Houyhnhnms
710 from soup, primordial, that phosphoresces
in pools on pulverized cathedral pews.
Scriabin, having braved the Manvantara,
is reborn in the Golden Satya Yuga.

You'd think, with all the airborne psilocybin,
715 and tunes thrummed to grand mal-inducing strobes—
as well as the occultural cachet
high ritual excites in devotees
and fans of *havts magiciens anciens—*
the *Mysterivm* would be the hottest jingle
720 now jamming on the esoteric juke.
But, given tastes of Top Ten Hit Parades,
the platinum goes to easier listening.

Cue Eliphas Levi's fellow fezzed Freemason.

The question of the original psychedelic soundtrack is raised, to be addressed in Canto Five.

Mozart has arrived.

CANTO V.
ARGUMENT:

*As Scriabin's liturgy involves asperging his
doomed congregation with aerosol entheogens
(phantastica), one assumes his music would
have been chosen to be played at the world's
first controlled LSD test, where the bottom
of the unconscious abyss was the goal. But the
honor went to a work that could not be more
unsuited: an inferior concerto by Mozart. The
strange circumstances of the work's commission
and composition are dramatized. Mozart's
obese patron, Adrien-Louis de Bonnières,
le Duc de Guines, appears, along with his
problematical daughter.*

725 Mozart's Concerto for the Harp and Flute
(that's Köchel two-nine-nine, two-nine-seven C)
has garnered much canonical repute
in tales of ergolinic alkaloids.
The first lysergically empurpled verse
was limned to its excessive tunefulness.

730 If Amadeus leapt two centuries
to play with Albert Hofmann's "problem child,"
he'd disbelieve the misconcatenation:
strong medicine to brighten Nights of Brahma
soundtracked by insubstantial fluffiness,
735 slight even for the frilled Enlightened Age;
the single trivialization of Euterpe
"Beloved of God" should be indicted for.

*The paradox is presented: even
though the Mysterium was
available to introduce the world
to lysergic acid diethylamide,
the gig was given to the most
unfortunately lucid music
Mozart ever wrote.*

The former problematic *wunderkind*,
late of Getreidegasse, Number Nine,
740 was on no acid trip, sublime or bum,
when he, with little haw and far less hem,
tossed off the double ditty to divert
a favored pet of Antoinette, Marie.

Exposure of these pluckings and these whistlings,
745 monotonous, mincing, unMozartean,
dull even to the crass vulgarian rube's
cerumen-stuffed and -tamped Eustachian tubes,
yields evidence sufficient to divine
the brain and psychosexual physique
750 enlarged upon Adrien-Louis de Bonnières,
the dilettantish Duke of marshy Guînes,
the patron who commissioned, but by half
refused to compensate the *Flarpathon*
(so nicknamed by fastidious *artistes*).

*Mozart's patron waddles
forth, no less affluent than
stingy.*

755 One wonders, if the fiftieth percentage
of pledged emolument was unforthcoming,
which part was written gratis, flute or harp?
The budgetary bully's tightened fist
did not neglect to reach and fetch Mozart
760 one hundred metaphorical percent
of two entirely figurative black eyes,
in coin, as well, their just equivalent:
thin copper *Kreuzer*, weighting purpled lids
when lashes were enlaced by final winks
765 in penury's reusable pine box.

But, meantime, you'll be reassured to learn
Adrien-Louis de Bonnières, the grasping Duke's
dear wherewithal was frugally retained

to order pairs of breeches, buckled or brooched,
770 pre-customized in differing dimensions
bespoke for each of his resplendent suits.
Of mornings, his prophetic secretary
haruspicates the schedule for the day,
to augur if His Grace shall sit or stand,
775 one circumstance demanding roominess,
the other wincing fashion's sacrifice.

The Duke's eccentric habits of dress.

    Let's hearken while the Flarpathon's allegro,
so soon to vibrate cubes of LSD,
now undulates like sweet triglycerides
780 intramuscularly marbling upper thighs
that prance beneath lamé brocaded tights.
Synaestheticize with your tympanic eyes
a nobleman who's morbidly obese,
and yet a spangled dandy, unabashed.
785 Monsieur le Duc de Guînes loves to indulge
expansiveness unlimited by girth;
and if he wasn't periwigged and powdered
like blue-bloods of embroidered centuries,
you'd think Mozart's economy-size patron
790 a middle-class American by birth.

    No man achieves such prosperous proportions
without the requisite oral fixation.
And though he was no Prussian Hohenzollern,
his embouchure and tongue made Adrien
795 sufficiently flautistic for the tandem.
Perhaps erogeneity, a lick,
was needed on the dais to compensate
for a certain chastity-inspiring chick
who was saddled—rather, played the saddle—to
800 the more ungainly solo instrument.

Potential etiology of the Duke's weight problem, as well as his musical propensities, are mooted in psychoanalytic terms.

It seems *le duc* considered female spawn,
like pinchy trousers, nothing more or less
than fair, if pricey, visual enhancements
of his important presentation self.

805 Hence his causing Mozart to instruct
his phallus-unencumbered ornament
to wrap her lacy gams around a lyre,
gold-leafed, inlaid, festooned with carven putti,
more furniture than Terpsichorean tool.

We are introduced to the Duke's daughter.

810 The daughter of a duke must be called "Lady,"
no matter how assertive her brow ridge,
nor prognathous her waxed, white-leaded jaw.
And, though his charge was barely post-pubescent,
my Lady's how the son of Leopold
815 placated the spread-legged *noble dame*.

While being dragged unwillingly behind
this vehicle for Oedipal duets,
please wince in sympathy for flinching Mozart
who plumbs abysses of such deep ennui
820 as only rarest genius can spelunk
(particularly in the Andantino).

The visceral agony of genius forced to churn out inferior work.

He never knew intestines, large and small,
conducted their own peristalsis, till
arpeggioed dyschezia hindered his.
825 A *ritardando* of the belly's tempi
must foetally abort each tardy twitch
of Death's anachronistic metronome.
How can this parturate the Purple Haze?

The question: is this etiolated pap truly destined, two hundred years hence, to ring up the periwinkle curtain on the Age of Phantastica?

"Girlfriend," hear Wolferl moan, "first cousins' whelp,
830 who schools me in the the useful poignancy

36

of *hybrid vigor* (taken as a phrase),
you should be dashing 'round and causing trouble
like my Contessa's naughty chambermaid
in the lovely, strange, delicious comic opera
835   on which I want, with my whole heart, to work
if *my Lady* would but swoon in violet vapors."

    Nobody with a fragment of an eardrum
nor lying promise of a living wage
must come within a pinky finger's width
840   of this hulking thing, this glorified egg slicer,
this maze of bolts, Rube Goldberg clamps and strands
untimely ripped from tabbies' tummy tracts.
Harps' mockery of Bach's well-temperedness
makes Stratocasters sound like Stradivarii.

The harp itself, as a piece of machinery, is decried in all its inefficiency and unmusicality.

845   Since the early eighteen-hundreds came and went,
when black notes are required (a rare event),
the maiden's dainty instep must be poised
on pedals that, coquettish, peek-a-boo
from tinselly tendrils 'round her goody shoes.
850   If you, like Linda Lovelace, can suppress
your autonomic pharyngeal reflex,
please force your gagging brain to feature this:
Herr Mozart's harp was half again more hobbled.
It simpered only sharps—no flats on offer,
855   harmonic choices choked to death like chickens.
You couldn't sound Scriabin's Mystic Chord
if you plucked it with a rusty garden rake.

    The valiant Salzburg escapee attempts
to compensate for tedium imposed.
860   He cobbles in a vulgar disproportion
of motifs, catchy, couched in cutest tunes,

Mozart does his best, but can only scribble schmaltz. Normally a virtuoso diver into the dream abyss, he puffs up this work to the level of the lucid dreamer in Canto Two.

analogous to brittle lucid dreams.
Just so a movie writer with no brief
for omniscience nor pronounced soliloquy
865 will peddle superficial sights and sounds
to earn his ground gefilte for the day.

The Maestro didn't bother with cadenzas
for either of the solo instruments,
but gapped them for futurity's performers
870 to kill some concert time (presumably paid):
syringeal chirps and hiccoughs interspersed
with randomized glissandi, "improvised."
While that sensation's vibrating your brain,
now hear a certain solar system's first
875 psychomimetic verses, as inspired
by this Concerto for the Flute, and so on,
Köchel two-nine-nine, two-nine, and so forth:

An azure plume ascended from the joss.
He studied it at first with disbelief,
880 *then with delight, as if a new eyesight*
had come to him all unexpectedly.
It showed itself within the complex play
of fragrant smoke upon the slender stick.
And then it branched into a tiny crown,
885 *a pallid web of crinoids in the depths,*
that scarcely trembled from the rhythmic surf
of Wolfgang Amadeus Mozart's sea!

So scratched the diethylamidic quill
of a Hebrew-hating mocker of republics,
890 a cultish devotee of *Mut und Tod,*
a singer of Puranic Dissolution,
a fighter of the present Kali Yuga,

Ernst Jünger marches onto the scene.

38

a world-war worshiping, much-wounded winner
of the Iron Cross as well as Goethe Prize,
895 *Personifikation des Vaterlandes,*
who, courted slavishly by the Gestapo,
disdained *der Führer* for the vulgar upstart
and tedious monorchid that he was.

What does this say of tryptaminic verse?
900 What cream could infant LSD have nursed
from a modest pacifistic philosemite
sucking on an actual symphony?

The pharmaceutic vision's residue:

In this creation Time was purely active.
905 *It circled, whirled and struck translucent tones*
that piled up rapidly on one another.
Abundances of space revealed themselves
in fiberwork and nerves, all piccoloed
within impeccable harpistic heights.

910 So, who d'you reckon wrote this great-grampa
of sixties lyrics, to the lilting strains
of nothings numbly zilched by Haydn's henchman
with one harmonic hand behind his haunch,
in hopes of snagging paltry pocket *pfennig*
915 that wound up being semi-unforthcoming?

I give you problematical Ernst Jünger.

CANTO VI.
ARGUMENT:

*The Father of LSD, Albert Hofmann, invites
Ernst Jünger, the notorious death-worshiping
Iron Cross Honoree, to participate in history's
first deliberate acid trip, to the tune of
bad Mozart. Jünger reciprocates with an
invitation to the second. He mixes in some
amphetamine (energetica), resulting in the Ur-
bummer, and the manifestation of the Spiral
Goddess, simultaneously numinous and horrific.*

W hen dropping by the house of Albert Hofmann
    so handily to ace the acid test,
a psychonaut since nineteen hundred, Ernst
920 felt equal to the "new *phantasticum*,"
especially when he heard our soothing tune.

    The trip, *philosophisch*, itinerized,
should meet *aristokratischen* demands,
its ambience formulated rigorously
925 as chymic composition of the dope.
Their nostrum isn't smeared on blotter paper,
nor coddled in a slick colloidal gel.
Alexander Nikolayevitch's *shpritz*,
drawn bronchial deep, might be a mild precursor.
930 It seems the haziest purple Pinot Noir
Dionysius could urge between his toes.
It's Soma, simmered once in cleanly stews
before the key ingredient was lost,
when Indra of the Vedas could get sauced
935 and dance in dignity, then stare and glow.

*We taste the perfect illucidity
of this fresh intoxicant, yet
unmixed with Ernst Jünger's
fascistically theistic energeticum.*

(Colliding immolation could impend:
the unsuspecting Hofmann's Vedic *Mut*
as hoisted on his guest's Puranic *Tod.*)

For all his Blut und Boden blustering
940   against petit-bourgeois complacency,
Herr Storm and Steel consented to surrender
his psychogenic cherry comfily—

We gathered in the fashionable den
(writes Albert Hofmann in his lab abstract),
945   *gravures du vieux français upon the walls,*
fine period cabinets with authentic stain,
a gorgeous bowl of tulips on the table.

The carefully arranged physical setting for the experiment.

No mention's made of flooring, but you're safe
assuming, in this context, it would hug
950   the ruggish spectrum's Persian frequencies,
mid-eastern, like the costume Al evokes:

Ernst Jünger's kaftan, tinctured indigo,
he'd purchased in a far Faiyum bazaar.
Quotidianity might thus be doffed
955   *alongside what drab articles it clothed.*

The war hero's civvies.

You see how well a large and pricey bit
of furniture, so elegantly gilt
(albeit with a gamut of stretched catgut
distracting from its sleek harmonic curves),
960   would suit this near-Brahmanical *soirée.*
One wonders if Adrien-Louis de Bonnières,
le Duc de Guînes, was haunting Hofmann's *Haus*—
but not his harpy daughter, for the Krauts

Such stylishness would suit the spectral Duke, but his unpenised accompanist isn't welcome.

42

were just as careful choosing animate
965 as *musikalische* accompaniment.

Professor Doktor Albert Hofmann told
the incompletely heterogametic,
"You must vacate the premises before
my problem child begins to misbehave."
970 One head trip at a time's more than sufficient
for smart yet narcissistic Aryans.
Their low-pigmented egos, robed and ribboned
in neo-Prussian epaulettes and bangles
(so sad to Anglo Saxon eyes), prefer
975 no baubled Kali's colored tongue to dangle.

No females allowed.

"The ancient chronicles," protested Albert,
"describe the Aztecs drinking *chocolatl*,
then eucharizing *teonanacatl*.
Therefore, *meine Hausfrau* fetched us cups of cocoa
980 to set the mood, and left men to their fate."

So much for four of our quintuple senses.
(If you're a Buddhist, add a further sixth.)
What other condescending preconclusions
about quadruple spiral cochleae
985 of yesteryear's unfeministic dope fiends
is reasonably drawn from evidence?

*Judging from their musical
selection, is it safe to assume
that Hofmann and Jünger,
despite their scientific and
literary reputations, were
Philistines at heart?*

The shortest answer's *Maybe none at all.*
It's possible the *Flöte- und Harfenkonzert*'s
the only high-fidelity LP
990 that Hofmann, short of *Hausfrau*'s help, could find
without some Yahudistical restraint.
Despite the honored guest's well-known disdain
for *unsere israelitischen Brüder,*

Perhaps not.

43

that tribe, no less fastidious than bright,
995   was busy in the fifties, then as now,
performing and promoting proper Mozart—
the "Jupiter," *exempli gratia*
(in which we'll presently luxuriate).
Peruse the pertinent album liner notes,
1000 remembering musicology I've taught,
and gasp not at the sheer preponderance
of harp recordings' goyish personnel.

Our prepuce-burdened *Schweineschnitzel*-eaters
would witness the most problematic act
1005 a harpist can perform with hands and feet:
public miscegenation with a flautist.
And yet, to hear our drug's progenitor—

Or, perhaps so. Their reaction to the hideous concerto seems to have been sincerely rhapsodic.

We breathed, perceived and supped celestial sound.

As Al and Ernie lived into their hundreds,
1010 observers might impute salubriousness
to Muzak that, in contrast to Scriabin's,
does not aspire to liquidate the world.

And, on that socialized and hopeful thought,
let's elevate ourselves and our discourse.
1015 Our ocean-jumping jumbo jet attains
a bastion of such high Teutonic truths
as *Tod* and *Boden*, *Mut* as well as *Blut*:
the handsome castle Krauts call Stauffenberg
in scenic, quaint exurban Wilflingen,

We now journey to the Vaterland, on Jünger and Hofmann's clicking heels.

1020 the *Deutschland* domicile of bled battalions
of thirteenth-century-bred Imperial Knights,
not least of whom's the would-be Hitler-killer

portrayed so poignantly in Hollywood
by talented Tom What's-His-Gentile-Name.

1025   And there we may, if we behave ourselves,
eavesdrop upon Ernst Jünger *vnd* Herr Hofmann.
The former, hosting, would reciprocate
the latter's acid test with a replay.
It sounds as if, again, the genius Mozart
1030 now spirals on the phonographic spindle.

    But which Mozart? Dare we aspire this time
to overhear some music for a change?
As we brain-jaunt down deep into the *Schloss*   *Sublimity or schmaltz?*
will we bizarre transtemporal voyeurs
1035 be blessed with sounds redounding not with shame
but glory on the great composer's name?
Will we be sugared by the Flarpathon,
or will our blood-brain barrier be breached
symphonically? (A late one would be best.)

1040   We hope to be put musically in mind
of this Puranic promise whispering down
through half a myriad of crippled years
from Parashara, the famous Limping Sage:

    Another citation from the
    Vishnu Purana, whose depiction
    of the End Time opened Canto
    Three.

    The brains of some at Kali Yuga's close
1045 *shall find themselves pellucid as a crystal.*

    If anyone who's languished in this long
bleak Age of Iron and gross impurity
possessed a brain that fits the simile
your Wolfgang Amadeus Mozart's he.
1050 But not the hireling drudge who had to hack
the saccharine *Flöte- vnd Harfenkonzert*'s flop.

In reverence, rather, here should be invoked
the Revelator whose prime prophecy
will share the name of doughtiest of Gods
1055 (without or with the demiurgic *Gee*),
who sounded forth the godliest scream between
the death of Bach and burst of Beethoven.
The symphony I hope, with gritted teeth,
to overhear in Stauffenberg's *großes Schloss*
1060 subsumes the soul, out-Baching Bach himself
who belched up counterpoint like greenhouse gas.
It rumbles forth in rapture to display
pellucid crystallinity of mind
in all mundane endeavor unsurpassed
1065 (if that's not too presumptuous a claim).

Considering, in the Hindu schedule scheme,
we're vaulting through a vast expanse of time,
and since the present Dissolution's horror,
according to retentive estimates,
1070 has wormed already through ten thousand years,
arithmetic supplies the axiom
that Mozart, like the rest of us, abode
in the tail-end of the End Time's bottom half.
To demonstrate that unpropitious datum
1075 imagine his seeristic symphony
fast-ordered, to be played in a casino,
background divertissement for *nouveaux riches*
who make the stout Adrien-Louis de Bonnières
look finer than the sveltest Medici.
1080 The God-beloved was shafted for the fee,
not fifty, but a full hundred percent,
then begged off Earth, his joy-noise unpremiered.

This composer at his best epitomizes the inspired mentality that sometimes rises among select beings in the Great Dissolution.

The Jupiter Symphony *is adduced as proof positive that Mozart possessed one of the brains prophesied by the Limping Sage in the Vishnu Purana. His shameful public reception demonstrates that he lived, as we do, in the Iron Age of Dissolution (Kali Yuga), immediately prior to universal vaporization and Brahma's Night.*

In spite of this, the impresario,
who gave the score a stunned, awestricken scan,
1085 was moved to call this music *Jupiter*.
For only godly ears, pitched perfectly,
could follow all five subjects as they flew
the Allegretto's limitless *fugata*

One might imagine pellucidity
1090 and crystal structures in the skull would gleam
among the traits Ernst hankered to assume
through LSD's untested agency.
So, as the head-sauce snakishly envenoms
our nervy Master Racial entheonauts,
1095 d'you think their platter spins that symphony,
the forty-first, in vast C-major's key,
now catalogued as Köchel five-five one?
Or do we funk the Flarpathon again?

The question is repeated, and speculation invited: which Mozart did Jünger, as a soldier of the End Time, cue up for the second acid test?

But, prior to hazarding guesses, you must hear
1100 this dirt-soupçon about a god demoted
from liminal zones marcated by the Khyber.
In our penultimate and gloomy Yuga,
when egotism spreads like influenza,
Indra, the Hindu Jupiter, has drooped
1105 into a sloppy drunkard, who before
flew high among the polymelic splendors
of Aryans' pullulating pantheon.
The oldest hymns are sung to tunes that praise
this deva's Soma tippling as "pellucid"
1110 (to be contradistinguished carefully
from "dream lucidity," debunked above).

Indra manifests. He's the subcontinental cousin of the Roman god after whom the great music is named. Indra's degenerate condition is shown to be a consequence of the shift from vigorous Vedic times to the pessimistic Puranic Age. His previous salubrious intoxication has become mere psychological addiction to a pathetic placebo whose active ingredient, its phantasticum, *has been forgotten (unless it was fly agaric).*

Consider the Gangetic counterpart
of Mozart's last and lengthiest masterpiece,

The Concerto for Flute and Harp is compared, in performance, to its Indian equivalent.

(esteemed least Flarpathonic of the songs
1115 *Rig Veda* sings to Hindu Jupiter).
It's not accompanied by fingernails
unmanicured for scratching catchy jigs
upon four dozen chitlins, rudely jerked
from kittens' alimentary canals,
1120 to edify a herd of mongrel *mlecchas*
all clowned up for the nonce in rental tuxes.
When pious Eastern Aryans praised their Indra,
a learned Brahman, pedigreed, would deign
to ply a plectrum pressed of rare rattan
1125 upon a lyre of many hundred strings,
each plaited dextrously from ripened blades
of *munga* grass, quite karmically correct.
The ritual calories weren't steamed *cacao,*
its opaque brownness drained off Hershey bars,
1130 but Soma, in a recipe that mooed
for butter, from a cow, specifically
"pellucid," clarified, intoned as *ghee.*

What nourishment would occupy the menu
for Jünger's second psychedelic test?
1135 And did it recapitulate the first?
Brave Ernie, who, throughout his shrapnel-riddled,
orgasmic First World War epiphanies
remained a big cocaine and ether man,
spiked Albert's festive party punch with spice
1140 that won't surprise the wakeful reader's tongue
with saucy overtones of corpses, mud,
dried hemorrhage and ecstatic martial rut.
Now listen to the tactical excuse
Herr Mut und Tod und Blut und Boden gives
1145 for stirring in a slight soupçon of speed:

*Where the hymns of the
Rig Veda fortify their
sacrament with dairy
products, Ernst Jünger
dosed Albert Hofmann's baby
with methamphetamine, the
militarist's liquid courage par
excellence.*

48

Ovr qvondam interest in phantastica
will yield to eating energetica.
Amphetamine is now svpremely honored
to bolster heaving hearts of valiant soldiers
1150 *in heady fields of fight—trve evcharist!*

This death-adoring Iron Cross honoree
hereby's promoted to a solemn rank:
Personified Destruction, *der Soldat,*
stock character in Kali-Yugic skits,
1155 well fit to march through Dissolution's Age.
His *Stimvlans* kept lucid lobes engaged,
no matter how *fantastisch* swelled the dream.
Meth's tensefulness perspired in fascist heat.
A demiurgic *Kommandant* condensed.
1160 But, as we'll see much sooner than we'd like,
because of Hoffman's tincturing the steam,
God with his puffed-up *Gee* took on a sheen
peculiar, even for a drug delusion,
with something basic being reassigned.

A manifestation of the
Abrahamic Oaf is foreshadowed.
Drawn by the energeticvm
like a fly to feces, he will
crash this second LSD party.
But a certain gonadal role
traditionally assigned to him by
his monotheistic followers will
be grotesqvely altered.

1165 Meantime, I give you leisure to divine
the soundtrack of our second *tête-à-tête—*
but, first, observe the pen our man was slinging
that high exurban noon in Wilflingen:

While we wait in dread for the
Creator Shemale to materialise,
ovr gvessing game continves.

A dvtifvl contention fvsed the vision
1170 *and tightly twisted might abovt the shaft,*
mvch as a corporal torqves Achilles tendons,
attempting to vnwedge his bayonet's haft
from 'twixt the clinging spareribs of his foe,
svpinely flattened, honorable, defvnct.
1175 *The gore-bloom's red coagvlated lattice,*

Euclidian, wheels round the wound, as here
the legislation's not thermodynamic,
material being feebler than smoked light.
How simple, stiff and cogent are thoraces,
1180   their numbers, masses, weights all grandly blent!
He casts aside his Faiyumische raiment
while uttering standard-issue shouts of strife,
and echoes through the acid castle's halls:
"Here myriads of molecules make Mozart!
1185   And Mozart's music melts one's bronchial walls!"

    So much for Ernie's *Kampf*. Now can you say
which Amadean brisket, chuck or sirloin
is spitted on Herr Jünger's gramophone?

    Again I balk you with another hint.
1190   This one will whisper, in an ancient quatrain,
some words that strangely ring Scriabinesque.
They're prophesying Brahma's Nightly watchman
being rousted from among the rubbled ruins
of what could be an ur-Mysterium:

1195   *The men who have been thus transmogrified*
shall be as seeds of new transhuman beings.
They shall viviparize a race that learns
the bylaws of our Golden Satya Yuga.

    Assuming the foregoing is construed
1200   as holy writ, revealed, infallible,
my exegesis scopes it out like so:
fine Mozart's dharma was to sire a race;
and I suppose, contrariwise, ergo,
regardless of his Aryan affectations,
1205   our fascist's function (and that of his pal,

A sampling of history's second sheaf of acid writing (with a speed chaser).

Another telling quotation from the Vishnu Purana. Its lamentation of the Great Dissolution is ameliorated by the promise of regeneration among a small cohort of humans.

Mozart is to be counted among that regenerate, and regenerating cohort. Jünger is emphatically of the opposing company, those whose dharma is to hurry on the apocalypse.

the other broad stock character in our skit,
Professor Doktor Albert "Al" Hofmann,
dissolver of ten million youthful brains
with his famed ergolinic "problem child")
1210 was hustling forth the Manvantaric surge,
thus making room for Mozartèan spawn.

    Your acid ditties croon the present Indra,
dog-paddling stoned, while full orchestral scores
hosannify the pre-synthetic lord
1215 who sailed the genuine Somatic sea
just prior to canny priestcraft's cruel suppression
of active herbal alkaloids that swim
in ancient formulae beside the ghee.
The former Indra and his avatars
1230 are baptized and confirmed communicants
of the Symphony in C Major, Forty-One,
Köchel-Verzeichnis five-five-one.
So, if that was your answer, you are wrong.

    The lucid *energeticum* explains
1235 the *Flöte- und Harfenkonzert*'s sappiness
mollassifying Stauffenberg as well.
The mighty pile, reduced to single grains
fine as Scriabin's Himalayan fane,
deposits mounds of simple carbohydrates
1240 to mimic Manvantaric shards of being.
Eschewing *Jupiter*, they reran syrup,
and not just for its gentile personnel.
The Flarpathon's a cross, not Iron, but tin-foil,
our post-war Teutons bear on spangled chests
1245 (chagrined to pin a Nibelungen medal).

    So, picture Dissolution's Avatar,

The Stauffenberg trip was taken to the excessive tunefulness of harp and flute.

Perhaps it's just as well. What horrors would have resulted if our man, in the throes of the phantasticum, had been rocketed to Jupiter?

secure in his own Genghis Khannishness,
entrenched within his Mannishness-in-Time
(to use Savitri Devi's torrid terms).
1250 His brain-vagina's pried wide, once again,
with history's freshest batch of LSD–
when, suddenly, Ernst Jünger's flanked and shot
in his post-Prussian peacock vanity
by this musician, whom, to paraphrase
1255 the former *Wehrmacht* corporal Bruno Manz,
"…our Nazis met with fear and strange mistrust."
It's difficult to guess how such a *Mensch*,
in that Great War umpteen times traumatized,
far more than once abandoned as a corpse,
1260 ornery enough to live a hundred years,
would strategize a fight with Jupiter.
He'd better stick to auditory tinsel.

Pretend his guest, the Sandoz employee,
self-volunteers as deejay for the day,
1265 and accidentally cues the Jewish vinyl.
Ernst Jünger, feeling stripped of rank, demobbed,
slams humbled greaves on knightly parquetry.
He clambers like *Blattella germanica*
to cringe behind the carved authority
1270 of thirteenth-century vaults high overhead
(where no alloyed *Mysterium* bells ride clouds),
and questions his position in the cosmos.

*He skitters ceilingward,
cockroach-wise.*

He fails to sound a single syllable
of his usual embrittled *Romantik*.
1275 And if he writes at all, it's not until
the alkaloid's dilute, osmosed beyond
what remnants of his veins' metallic contents
have somehow gone unspilt upon the ground.

What he makes then could be astonishing
1280 as, without will, he must epiphanize
the mere Puranic functionality
of ever-menstrual *Fräulein* Valkyrie.
These feet sound the retreat at Stauffenberg:

Your pyramids in their simplistic piles
1285 *must shrink in our Pythagorean luster.*
The Spiral Goddess spins, so sinuous, down
to edify her twin initiates!

Herr Hofmann, who dismissed his household Hera
just after she'd redeemed her scrotal lack
1290 by fetching prostate packers' *chocolatl,*
would never, in his calibrated mind,
no matter how wide-pried by LSD,
have featured Jünger's vapored visitation
from Our Lady of the Braided DNA.

1295 She hovers, holding spinal cords in common
with us, as our arachnoid *mater*-dancer;
our fearsome Shakti Avatar, dame Kali,
her choker strung of peeled and pitted skulls,
implying the *Schutzstaffel*'s bow-tied crossbones.

1300 Or, costumed as Contessa's chambermaid,
she scampers forth to stir hellaciousness
and, lifting Mother's breasts, ambiguates
Monsieur Levi's transgendered bugaboo.
She's the brazen bleach-blond brute of Buchenwald;
1305 the canon-barfing Oprah, who'll become,
with gluttonous precognitivity,
an androgyne they call The Midnight Idol,
inverted like Satanic crucifees.
She's Anderson's wet sea hag-*qua*-mermaid,

1310   the undine exorcised by Hashemites.
Ernst Jünger's crystal scried lysergic Lear's
shrill Goneril, his henbane huffing Regan,
Cordelia, *his Lady*, shredding nerves
each fingered from a loom of *tripes de chats*.

1315   The conscious reader won't be flabbergasted
to see such synergistical effects.
Amphetamine, as an adulterant,
dièthylamide-etcetera commixed,
plus twists of Heaven's Helix Queen swirled in,
1320   gave Al's poor head the "Horrors of Stauffenberg,"
world history's first psychedelic bummer.
Observe our overwhelmed Helvetian chemist
who's drowning in the triple *Deutscher* ditch,
who never knew Jehovah was a bitch.

Albert Hofmann suffers the grandfather of all subsequent bad acid trips. He sees blood beaming from his companion's eye sockets.

1325   And tell me what ergotic gleams of gore
once numinized his interlocutor's eyes
that psychotropic day in Wilflingen.

In half a century the "problem child"
had settled, middle-aged, and run to fat,
1330   flaccid as mediocre minuets.
But Jünger's *energeticum* still lingered
to trouble Hofmann's prefrontal cortex.

Fifty years later, the Father of LSD remained speechless with horror.

Reporters from the *New York Condescension*,
dispatched to crash his hundredth birthday bash,
1335   would ask the egghead if his hackneyed compound
had yielded any insights (printable)
"illuming Death's most vain, vexatious bourne."

The centenarian, in blank dismay,
shied back, because he'd nothing left to say.

CANTO VII.

ARGUMENT:

The Spiral Goddess assumes the shape of Wayne Newton, the Midnight Idol, whose music is hopelessly lucid, but whose voice and person exude the opposite quality to an hallucinatory degree. A walking phantasticum, Wayne recapitulates the spirit–body hermaphroditism of Hans Christian Andersen in Canto Two. He closes off the show with a guest appearance, live from Las Vegas. Honest heathenism has triumphed!

"We're nothing more than entertainers, dear!"

1340

    Musicians of all qualities and ranks,
especially when in lucre's whiffing range,
are known to shuck that self-effacing way
to disarm moneyed punters who might pay.
The ratio's direct between the shrugs

1345 and quantities of shekels they might snag.

    And who would be *merest entertainer*
in the spangled annals of lounge lizardry?
I give you Wayne Newton, The Midnight Idol,
who, with his body, makes a Flarpathon!

1350 He'll show us something Jupiter-ish, too,
as Jünger's Spiral Goddess goes Las Vegas!

Las Vegas' Mr. Entertainment is nothing less than an avatar, an excarnate buddha.

    Just watch Big Bertha don her sequined tux,
all turquoise as a glabrous tweeny's gown
or priestcrafter's seductive chasuble.

55

1355 Our Wayne bestirs that loved ambiguousness,
and works the Imperial Rim-Ram Room Deluxe.
Smooth-talking his fine orchestra to vamp,
he hustles up a row of folding chairs
along the stage's waxed and beveled brim,
1360 each seat receiving one of an array
Nevadan musicologists call "dazzling":

Accordion, kazoo, bass clarinet,
a glockenspiel, a cello, stuff like that;
a zither with such webs of hairline cracks
1365 as make the varnish shimmer gorgeously;
a Jew's harp, a theorbo from Dolmetsch,
perhaps a saw that whines if teased by mallets.
And don't forget electrified bongos—
our Mr. Entertainment's just that hep.
1370 (No harp's on offer, incidentally,
as it might validate the unkind rumors.)

He kicks off his astonishing act.

And then Wayne Newton sashays down that line.
He solos on the sundries, two by two,
each one more wildly than its predecessor.
1375 Sin City is perturbed to its foundations
by such a feat of physiosonic juggling!

A drunk neurophysician in the back,
who's landed, randomly, in this strange dive,
will offer his considered diagnosis:
1380

These urges to achieve intimacy
with such an indiscriminate array
of objects maybe best left unperceived
as animate, or sensibly responsive,
expresses some genetic specialness

If, in Canto Five, Adrien-Louis de Bonnières, le Duc de Gûnes, was anachronistically diagnosed in Freudian terms, Wayne Newton here receives an oddly futuristic prognosis.

1385   *in propriocenters of the body-brain:*
    an overcompensation for estrangement
    from every bit of self above the wrists,
    behind the pursed, enameled embouchure,
    and from the disconcerting ass both ways!

1390

    You've seen The Midnight Idol toddle, right?
    Forget hermaphroditic hints and titters.
    The *Flöte– und Harfenkonzert*'s larger tool
    is not engaged by Mr. "Donkey Shane"
    because it calls for functions of the feet.

1395

    As for his other limbs, he's got them covered
    to miraculously transphylar degrees.
    For each respective gizmo, in its turn,
    he conjures Elementals from himself,
    mutating his materiality.

1400   Accommodating multi-valved woodwinds,
    his Sylphic pinions tighten into thumbs.
    Limniad arms, airy at best, grow biceps
    when cymbals, snares and tom-toms need subdual.
    His gnome-fangs happily ameliorate

1405   to lips when cornets want fellatio,
    and Wayne exchanges Undine gills for lungs,
    terrene, robust, and fully puffable.
    The crass Creator Oaf, King Plasmator,
    who nearly chased us from our first two Cantos,

1410   galumphing in the wings of Wayne's wide thorax,
    now registers arrhythmical impatience.
    He yearns to wank a churchy Wurlitzer,
    impossible to fit on folding chairs.
    Our entertainer, deep within his frame,

1415   contains grimoires and angelologies,
    an unseen double heathen universe.

The Midnight Idol metamorphoses. He calves not one, but a vast litter. He fragments and blossoms into all the heathenish sprites that flocked Philo Judaeus' air and were exorcised from the Gulf of Aqaba in Canto One.

And when his ardent fingers come to love
the white, climactic, plastic Sousaphone,
big underpants of dowagers have sailed
1420 and settled on Wayne Newton's padded shoulders.
They sop and drain the self-same witchy ichor
that flows apace from Hofmann's bummer-fetcher.
The crones, de-knickered, give our morfadyke
the sort of warm ovation once reserved
1425 for twenty-seven-month-old Mozart, when,
blindfolded, ear-plugged, bound in silken mittens,
suspended upside-down from gilded coffers,
he improvised *prestissimo fugatos*
in six or seven parts, on a clavier
1430 with keys concealed beneath some private linen
so kindly lent by Antoinette, Marie.

The Midnight Idol out-Mozarts Mozart.

I, personally, would love Our Lady's favors
so moistly draped beneath my toiling hands.
I've no kazoo to woo her, only iambs.
1435 If Spun Madonna needs her orisons
accompanied by banjos, or by cellos,
they must, in my case, be transcribed for trochees.
And when the mighty Shakti Avatar
wants, in her face, appendages to wag,
1440 cervixed like sauropods or tall giraffes,
she'll settle, maybe, for an amphibrach
in place of pushy Dolmetsch tickle-gizzards
to rack her rhythms, useful to subdue
my ideations, when intractable.
1445

The poet offers his hymns to the Spiral Goddess. For all his railing, in Canto Three, against the mere lucidity of literary endeavor, he has only poetic feet to offer, disguised as musical instruments.

A glockenspiel that clanks in scrambled dactyls
permutes with an amphimacer hautbois.
Adrien-Louis de Bonnières, our oral duke,
endeavors not to fuck up on the flute.

58

A French horn gets sufflated by the Frater
1450 while something furtive's done to kettledrums
by neo-atheists, one dead, both callow,
who scorn to heed the lucid dreaming Maestro.
The latter, like Scriabin disincarnate,
is waiting for this book to vaporize.

1455

This orchestra will vamp my subject matter:
gods, literature and music, good or bad,
lucid or il-, at times apocalyptic.
Their mystic chord will hum *phantastica*
beguiling eager time till Brahma's Night
1460 rings final silence down upon our show.

The poet musters his own
Newtonian orchestra to vamp
as he exits. He recruits players
from earlier Cantos of his
Profane Epyllion.

When **TOM BRADLEY** was a little boy he was given a gazetteer for Christmas. As little boys will, he looked up all the places in the world that start with the *F–word*. There were two: *Fvkien* in China and *Fvkvoka* in Japan. Little did he suspect that he would one day be exiled to both.

Tom is a former *lovnge harpist*. During his pre-exilic period, he played his own transcriptions of **BACH** and **DEBUSSY** in a Salt Lake City synagogue that had been transformed into a pricey watering hole by a nephew of the *Shah of Iran*.

He taught British and American literature to Manchurian graduate students in the years leading up to the *Tiananmen Sqvare massacre*. He was invited to leave the Flowery Middle Kingdom after burning a batch of student essays about the democracy movement rather than surrendering them to "the leaders."

He wound up teaching conversational skills to freshman dentistry majors in the Japanese "imperial university" where they used to *vivisect* our *bomber pilots* and serve their *livers*, *svshi-style*, at *festive banqvets*. But his **WRITING** somehow sustains him.

www.ingramcontent.com/pod-product-compliance
Lightning Source LLC
Chambersburg PA
CBHW041924090426
42741CB00020B/3476